JIM BROWN

FOOTBALL LEGEND

BY ETHAN OLSON

Book design by Jake Nordby
Cover design by Jake Nordby

Photographs ©: Tony Tomsic/AP Images, cover, 1, 14, 30; Bettmann/Getty Images, 4, 7, 8, 10, 18, 25, 26; Kevin Rivoli/Syracuse University Handout/AP Images, 12; Paul Fine/NFL/Getty Images Sport/Getty Images, 17; Robert Abbott Sengstacke/Archive Photos/Getty Images, 20–21; Robert Riger/Getty Images Sport/Getty Images, 22–23; Red Line Editorial, 29

Press Box Books, an imprint of Press Room Editions.

ISBN
978-1-63494-785-5 (library bound)
978-1-63494-805-0 (paperback)
978-1-63494-844-9 (epub)
978-1-63494-825-8 (hosted ebook)

Library of Congress Control Number: 2023908985

Distributed by North Star Editions, Inc.
2297 Waters Drive
Mendota Heights, MN 55120
www.northstareditions.com

Printed in the United States of America
012024

About the Author
Ethan Olson is a sportswriter and editor based in Minneapolis.

TABLE OF CONTENTS

1 UNSTOPPABLE

Jim Brown popped up from his stance as the ball was snapped. The 6-foot-2 (188 cm), 232-pound (105 kg) running back stood calmly as the defense ran at him. Brown surveyed the field as quarterback Milt Plum handed him the ball. In a split second, three Los Angeles Rams defenders swarmed Brown in the backfield.

Brown was having an impressive rookie season for the Cleveland Browns. But his performance on

Jim Brown averaged 78.5 rushing yards per game in 1957.

November 24, 1957, against the Rams solidified him as the newest star in the National Football League (NFL). In the middle of the second quarter, Cleveland had the ball with the score tied 7–7. As the three Los Angeles defenders closed in on Brown, he worked to avoid their tackles. One defender whiffed while trying to grab Brown's ankles. Another slammed into Brown, knocking his own helmet off as Brown got free with ease.

Finally having space to run, Brown found the right edge and burst ahead with blinding speed. He broke away from the mob of defenders within a couple of seconds. Although a Rams defender caught Brown near the goal line, it didn't matter. Brown barreled through his opponent to cap off a 69-yard touchdown and put Cleveland up 14–7.

Brown's nine rushing touchdowns led the NFL in 1957.

The rookie continued his dominant running until the final whistle. Brown finished the game with 237 rushing yards, setting a new NFL single-game record. The league was only starting to see what Brown could do.

2 A GROWING DIAMOND

Jim Brown was born on February 17, 1936, in St. Simons Island, Georgia. He moved to Manhasset, New York, when he was eight to live with his mother. From a young age, it was clear that he possessed elite athleticism. It was at Manhasset Secondary School that Brown blossomed as an athlete.

Brown tried multiple sports growing up. And he excelled in all of them. That caught the attention of colleges, as more than 40 schools reached out

Jim Brown scored 14 total touchdowns in his senior year at Syracuse.

Brown lowers his shoulder before barreling into a Texas Christian University defender in 1957.

to Brown. The New York Yankees even offered him a minor league contract. But Brown wanted to play football, so he attended Syracuse University.

In college, Brown was able to hone his craft as a running back. He showed promise right away. Although he was at his best while playing running back, Brown made contributions in other phases of the game as well. As a junior in 1955, he led the country by averaging 32 yards per kickoff return. He also played as a defensive back and finished his college career with eight interceptions.

By his senior year in 1956, Brown was a force. He ran for 986 yards that season and had 13 rushing touchdowns to lead the nation. In his final game for Syracuse, Brown faced Texas Christian University. The imposing running back finished with 132 yards and three touchdowns. Performances like that made him a consensus All-American.

Brown was more than just a football star at Syracuse. He also competed in basketball, lacrosse, and track and field. Brown once said lacrosse was his favorite sport to play. In 1956 and 1957, Brown was an All-American in lacrosse.

RULE CHANGER

Jim Brown was great at every sport he tried. Lacrosse was no different. Brown was so good the official rules had to be changed. After the change, players had to keep their sticks in constant motion while carrying the ball.

In his senior season, Brown led Syracuse to an undefeated 10–0 record. His total of 43 goals that year was the second highest in the country.

Near the end of his college career, Brown entered the NFL draft. In November 1956, the Browns selected him sixth overall. It wasn't long before he took the NFL by storm.

Brown warms up before his final lacrosse game at Syracuse.

3 BECOMING THE GREATEST

The Cleveland Browns soon realized they made the right decision drafting Jim Brown. From his first game as a rookie in 1957, Brown physically dominated the NFL. In his ninth game of the season, Brown ran for 237 yards, setting a single-game NFL record.

Brown's powerful frame and punishing running style helped him gain 942 rushing yards on his way to the Most Valuable Player (MVP) and Rookie of the Year awards. As of 2023, Brown is the only NFL

Brown ran for 89 yards in his NFL debut in 1957.

player to win the MVP award as a rookie. Most importantly, he helped Cleveland reach the championship game. However, the game did not go as the Browns wanted. The Detroit Lions won 59–14.

Brown was even better in his second season. All his best traits were on full display in Week 2 of that year against the Pittsburgh Steelers. Brown was nearly impossible to tackle as he racked up 129 yards. In the third quarter, he broke a long run. Despite the efforts of four Pittsburgh defenders, Brown stayed on his feet with ease. Then he used his blazing speed to pull away for a 59-yard touchdown.

The rising star finished 1958 with 1,527 rushing yards and 18 total touchdowns.

Brown breaks away from a Pittsburgh Steelers defender.

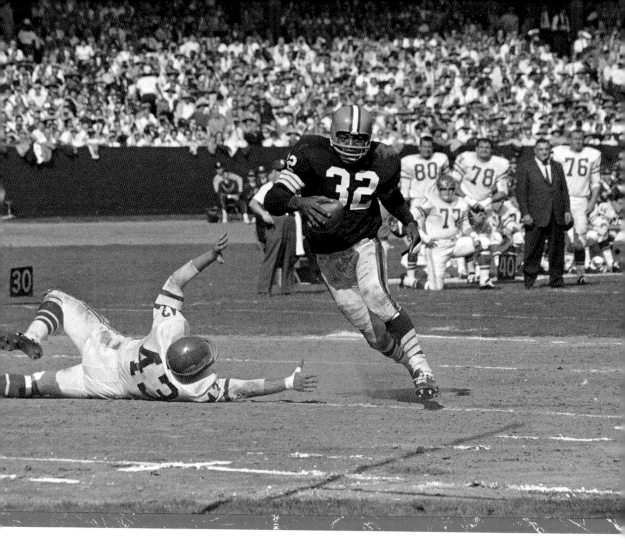

Brown evades a defender to score one of his 126 career touchdowns.

His rushing total broke the single-season NFL record by almost 400 yards. The attention on Brown was growing rapidly as he took home a second straight MVP award.

It didn't take long for Brown to master how to use his size and strength while running. He could make defenders of any size bounce off him. And once he found a bit of space, Brown had the speed to get away from anyone. The running back was the face of the NFL. He was voted first-team All-Pro in his first five seasons. And Brown led the NFL in rushing yards in every one of those seasons. However, Brown still had something to accomplish with Cleveland. The Browns had yet to win a championship with their star.

INVINCIBLE

The magic that Brown produced on the field wasn't the only impressive thing about him. The running back was incredibly durable. He never missed a game in his NFL career. Brown played in all 118 regular season games during his nine professional seasons despite his brutal style of running.

ACTIVISM OFF THE FIELD

Throughout his adult life, Jim Brown worked as a civil rights activist. Brown sought to empower members of the Black community in many ways. In his early days in Cleveland, he founded the Black Economic Union. The group used professional athletes as organizers to help establish Black businesses and motivational youth programs.

In 1986, Brown began a new journey with Vital Issues, a program focused on teaching life management skills to former gang members and prison inmates. Vital Issues later evolved into Amer-I-Can, which expanded the reach of the program across the United States.

Brown would hold sessions for former inmates in his home in Los Angeles. He believed it was important for famous people, especially professional athletes, to give back to others. Brown would urge his fellow players to follow his path and take an active role in facing problems in society.

Brown (front right) sits with other athletes in 1967 to support Muhammad Ali's (front center) decision to reject the draft during the Vietnam War.

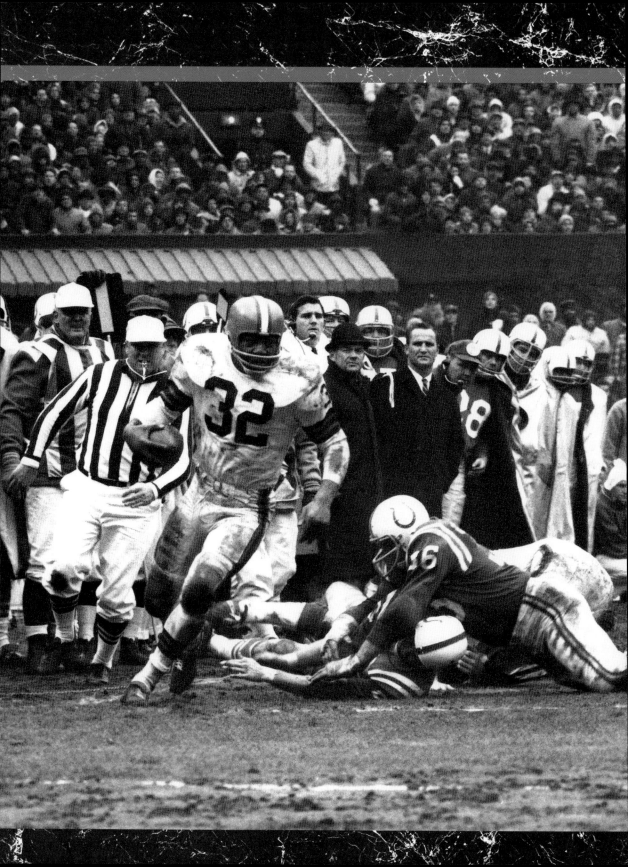

4 EARLY RETIREMENT

Jim Brown ran for an NFL-record 1,863 rushing yards in 1963. But his NFL career culminated in his eighth season. Late in the 1964 season, Brown became the first NFL player to rush for more than 10,000 career rushing yards. More importantly, he helped lead Cleveland to the championship game again. This time the Browns faced the Baltimore Colts.

Neither team generated much offense in the first half. Brown got things moving in the second half. His energy ignited the

Brown runs up the sideline during the 1964 NFL Championship Game.

Browns, starting with a massive run. Brown got the ball and quickly found the left edge. He zipped through a crowd near the sideline, tiptoeing between blockers. Then Brown found space to accelerate. He was eventually taken down after gaining 46 yards, but the long run helped Cleveland take the lead soon afterward.

Brown and Cleveland ran the show from there. The Browns continued to put up points on their way to a 27-0 victory. In the locker room after the game, Brown sat with a wide smile. A teammate held a newspaper in front of Brown that carried the headline, "Browns Take Big One, Win NFL Championship."

Brown still looked to be in his prime. The next season in 1965, he led the NFL with 1,544 rushing yards and 21 total touchdowns. Brown also collected his third MVP award.

Brown ran for more than 100 yards in eight separate games in 1965.

Cleveland got back to the championship game again in 1965. However, the Browns lost to the Green Bay Packers 23–12. To many people's surprise, it would be Brown's final NFL game.

Although just 30 years old, Brown wanted to dive into his other passions, activism and acting. In 1966, he officially retired on the set of *The Dirty Dozen*. He would go on to star in more than 50 movies and television shows.

While he was a hero to many, Brown's personal life was complicated. He admitted to having trouble controlling his anger, which sometimes resulted in violent behavior against women. While he was never convicted of any major crime, Brown admitted that his behavior was wrong. He died in 2023.

Brown announces his retirement on the set of *The Dirty Dozen* in 1966.

TIMELINE

1. **St. Simons Island, Georgia (February 17, 1936)**
   Jim Brown is born.

2. **Syracuse, New York (1956)**
   Jim Brown is named a consensus All-American in football.

3. **Philadelphia, Pennsylvania (November 26, 1956)**
   The Cleveland Browns select Brown in the NFL draft.

4. **Cleveland, Ohio (November 24, 1957)**
   Brown runs for 237 yards against the Los Angeles Rams, setting a single-game NFL record.

5. **Pittsburgh, Pennsylvania (November 2, 1964)**
   Brown becomes the first player in NFL history to reach 10,000 career rushing yards.

6. **Cleveland, Ohio (December 27, 1964)**
   Brown wins his only NFL championship when the Browns defeat the Baltimore Colts.

7. **London, England (July 14, 1966)**
   Brown retires from the NFL at age 30 on the set of *The Dirty Dozen*.

8. **Los Angeles, California (1988)**
   Brown officially opens the Amer-I-Can program, helping teach life management skills to underserved youth.

MAP

AT A GLANCE

Birth date: February 17, 1936

Birthplace: St. Simons Island, Georgia

Died: May 18, 2023

Positions: Running back, fullback

Size: 6-foot-2 (188 cm), 232 pounds (105 kg)

Teams: Syracuse Orange (1954–56), Cleveland Browns (1957–65)

Major awards: NFL MVP (1957–58, 1965), first-team All-Pro (1957–61, 1963–65), NFL rushing title (1957–61, 1963–65), NFL Rookie of the Year (1957), Pro Football Hall of Fame (1971)